All for Oil

By the same author

Poetry
Poems — Ibari
A Reed in the Tide — Longman
Casualities — Longman
A Decade of Tongues — Longman
State of the Union — Longman
Mandela and other Poems — Longman
A Lot from Paradise — Malthouse

Drama
Three Plays: Songs of a Goat
           The Masquerade
           The Raft — Oxford
Ozidi — Oxford
The Bikoroa Plays: The Boat — Oxford
                    The Return Home
                    Full Circle
The Wives' Revolt

Criticism
The Example of Shakespeare — Longman
The Hero as a Villain — Lagos

Travel
America, their America — Andre Deutsh

Research and Translation
The Ozidi Saga — Oxford
                  Ibadan

American Editions
Collected Plays and Poems — Howard UP
The Ozidi Saga — Howard UP

All for Oil

J. P. Clark

Malthouse Press Limited

Malthouse Press Limited
8 Amore Street, Off Toyin Street,
PO Box 500, Ikeja, Lagos State, Nigeria

Lagos, Benin, Ibadan, Jos, Oxford, Port-Harcourt, Zaria

All rights reserved. No part of this publication may be reproduced, stored in a retrieval system, or transmitted, in any form or by any means, electronic, mechanical, photocopying, recording, or otherwise, without the prior permission in writing of Malthouse Press Limited.

This book is sold subject to the condition that it shall not, by way of trade or otherwise, be lent, re-sold, hired out, or otherwise circulated without the publisher's prior consent, in writing, in any form of binding or cover other than that in which it is published and without a similar condition including this condition being imposed on the subsequent purchaser.

© J.P. Clark 2000
First Published 2000
ISBN 978 023 132 3
ISBN-13: 978-978-023-132-3

All production enquiries should be directed to the playwright through the publisher.

The setting

In the European scramble for Africa towards the end of the 19th century, Britain declared for itself the Oil Rivers Protectorate to gain monopoly of the palm oil trade in what is now part of the land it put together as a country. Later, it formed the first Federation of Nigeria with the former Royal Niger Company as its principal commercial operator, and the indigenous people of the area, the Niger Delta, the suppliers of the raw materials that Britain needed for its factories.

Today, at the beginning of the 21st century, oil again, this time, petroleum, has been for years the one major commodity making up Nigeria's economy, and indeed the reason for its existence. The players, as in the story before, are the same, namely, the Nigerian State, run by the majority ethnic groups to whom Britain ceded it at independence; the economic partners are the multinational oil companies; and at the bottom of the heap, in the heart of the old Oil Rivers Protectorate, the people of the Niger Delta, left squabbling among themselves by the Lugardian policy of divide-and-rule.

Drawing upon official colonial documents and oral tradition, *All for Oil*, presents a powerful panorama of the players in the original drama of the creation of Nigeria. Sir (later Lord) Frederick Lugard and Colonel M.C. Moorhouse, aided by Chief Dore Numa, a local agent for the British in their wars of aggression against Nana Olomu the Itsekiri (1894) and Oba Ovonramwen of Benin (1897), represent the colonial administration; the Niger Company dominates the trade; and "its largest trade and middleman" in the Western Niger Delta, Chief Bekederemo (Ambakederemo), his friend, Chief Egbe, and his lawyer, Egerton Shyngle, Leader of the Nigerian Bar and First Elected Member, the Legislative Council of Nigeria, 1923-1926, give voice to the interests and yearnings of the local people as it has never been heard and reported before in the presentation of Nigeria's history.

Oil, the issue facing a country calling today for urgent restructuring so that it may survive, burns through the scenes of this drama in which the mind of a master truly matches the matter.

All for Oil is a play for our present times of crisis after crisis, a play for all who really care that this volatile resource is responsibly and properly managed for peace and prosperity to prevail in our land.

All for Oil was first presented at the Institute of Church and Society, Ibadan on 18 September, 2000; at Obafemi Awolowo University, Ile-Ife on 19 and 20 September, 2000; at the Arts Theatre, University of Ibadan, Ibadan on 23 September, 2000; at the Greetings Hall, Yoruba Tennis Club, Lagos on 27 September, 2000; at the National Theatre, Lagos on 28 September, 2000 and at the Kuto Cultural Centre, Abeokuta on 10 October, 2000 by PEC Repertory Theatre in association with the University of Ibadan Department of Theatre Arts with a cast and production crew featuring for the first time the U.I. Holiday Players:

Chief Bekederemo (Ambakederemo), 'the largest trader and middleman for the Niger Company in the Western Niger Delta at the beginning of the 20th century.

    Osa Ogunmu
    Patrick Eichie
    Tunde Onikoyi

Mitovwodo, his senior wife

    Sherifa Ikhazs
    Bukky Badeji
    Nimibofa Ozigbo
    Peace Omowaiye
    Abiola Agunloye
    Ruth Epochi
    Dupe Kamiyole

Fuludu, his first son and heir

    Emmanuel Nlemadin
    Akin Oyeleke
    Anthony Konwea

Nemugha, his adviser from youth

    Tony Ekoh
    Jude Udueni
    Ben Iwuala

Branuvwere, his old bondsman

    Daddy Ejidoh
    Gafar Ajao

Piniki Ederume, his bard

    Tunde Onikoyi
    Jide Ali
    Samsideen Adesiyan

Egerton Shyngle, leader of the Nigerian Bar and First Elected Member, Legislative Council of Nigeria, 1923-1926, his lawyer.

Nash Odigie
Moyo Osundare
Bimbo Benson

Chief Dore Numa: British Political Agent on the Benin and Warri Rivers and unofficial Member for Warri in the Nigeria Council, after serving with the British in their Wars against Nana the Itsekiri in 1894 and Oba Ovonramwen of Benin in 1897.

Ben Iwuala
Adebayo Alawiye
Patrick Eichie

Bar Rolle, Court Clerk

Gabrielle Ojo
Temitope Akanbi Sugar
Ayo Atom Adewumi

Court Messenger

Gboyega Aminu
Akinola Olanrewaju

S. L. Bucknor, lawyer for Chief Dore

Tolulope Olusanya
Kehinde Olakpe
Fashola Igbagbolere
Christian Onyedinachi

Chief Babigha, Dore's father-in-law

Moshood Folorunsho
Bisi Madamidola
Wale Adebayo

Fetaroro, his son

James Famoriyo
Jude Udueni
Akin Oyeleke

Chief Egbe, Bekederemo's friend and brother-in-law

Kayode Somoye
Paul Emokhare
Ayo Atom Adewumi

Fiobode, his wife

Lara Lawal
Dupe Kamiyole
Joy Osanekwu
Bunmi Wuraola
Toyin Edalere
Ruth Epochi
Bisi Madamidola

Johnson Nana, son of Nana the Itsekiri	Konwea Anthony Emmanuel Nlemadin Igbagbolere Fashol
Col M.C. Moorhouse, Officer Administering the Government of Nigeria in the absence of Sir (later Lord) Frederick Lugard, Governor-General and Commander-in-Chief	Kayode Ogunyemi Tunde Onikoyi
Mr. (later Sir) A.C. Burns, Political Secretary, in the Office of the Governor-General of Nigeria.	Kola Ogunyemi Samsideen Adesiyan

Director	Dapo Adelugba
Set Design	Demas Nwoko
Set Construction	J. C. Aborisade
Publicity	Tunde Onikoyi Samsideen Adesiyan Ayo Atom Adewunmi Akinola Olanrewaju
Box Office	Lara Lawal Bunmi Wuraola Sherifat Ikhazs Peace Omowaiye
Business Management	Nimibofa Ozigbo Kayode Somoye
Props Management *Assisted by*	Gafar Ajao Kehinde Olakpe
Costume/Makeup *Assisted by*	Bukky Badeji Joy Osanekwu Dupe Kamiyole
Computer Graphics	Gafar Ajao
Stage Management	Paul Emokhare Ben Iwuala

Assistant stage managers	Akin Oyeleke
	Peace Omowaiye
	Fashola Igbagbolere
	Konwea Anthony
Production Management	Kayode Shomoye
	Daddy Ejidoh
Music	Lekan Adedokun
	Kolape Akinola
Diary	Jude Udueni
Set and Light	Hanson Okoh
Training Sessions	Kayode Somoye
	Nimibofa Ozigbo
	Paul Emokhare
	Tony Ekoh
	Ben Iwuala
	Daddy Ejidoh
	Gafar Ajao
	James Famoriyo
	Bukky Badeji
Consultants	Taiwo Ajayi Lycett
	Duro Oni
	Dr Chris Nabofa
	Dr J. E. Ifie
	David & Kathy Okpako

Note: Bekederemo and Dore are Anglicized forms of the Izon name Ambakederemo and the Itsekiri name Dogho, retained here in essential places for reasons of maintaining consistency with existing colonial documents. Similarly, the forms Ijo, Ijaw for Izon; Sobo for Urhobo, and Jekri for Itsekiri.

Director's note: Multiple cast
The first production of *All for Oil* was prepared during the Long Vacation (July – September) of the University of Ibadan in 2000. To give maximum opportunities to the large number of talented actors and actresses who deserved to perform this eighteen-character play (in terms of speaking parts), it was made to involve a cast of about fifty persons. Each role was therefore, as rehearsal progressed, double-cast or triple-cast

and, in some cases (especially the female roles which were few) quadruple-cast or multiple-cast.

Each actor in each role considered this a golden opportunity to develop his or her talent to the full and audiences who saw the production on more than one night have attested to the success of the multiple-casting system evolved for the maiden production of *All for Oil*.

The multiple-casting system was not a mere ploy to cater for the numbers of talented persons in the company. The more flexible actors and actresses, indeed, were able to tackle more than one role in a production which is billed to be performed in many towns and cities all over Nigeria and, hopefully, beyond our shores.

I

Regatta and after

Sometime between 1912 and 1915. At Ugbanwengwe, in the compound of Chief Egbe, outside the new township of Warri, after a regatta on the Warri River for Sir (later Lord) Frederick Lugard, Governor-General and Commander-in-Chief of the newly amalgamated British protectorate that his wife has just named Nigeria, on tour of the Southern Provinces.

Chief Bekederemo and his host and brother-in-law, Chief Egbe, both in ceremonial dress of the time, have just returned from the state occasion. He is trying to get out of his gear as soon as he steps into the veranda of his friend's house, calling out at the same time for food for his men and himself. Between both demands, his brother-in-law and his sister, Fiobode, are doing their best to make him comfortable.

Bekederemo: Come, come, Egbe, where is the food? Asagba and his crew want to catch the ebb tide home. Do you see how the white man has piled our plate full with problems? He has summoned a whole crowd of people, big and small, each speaking a different tongue, into a single hall, which he calls Nigeria. How are we going to hear each other speak? And above all the din, he hands us a song to sing at gun-point. We are in trouble, my brother.

Egbe: Yes, yes, but let's see about your food first. Fiobode, where are you?

Fiobode: Right by your side. It's all nearly done. In fact, the men have been served. But these coral beads must not be left lying around – and of course, the gold chains. Let me help you, my one and only brother. Your men are quite happy outside, laughing and fighting over their food and drinks.

Egbe: What a crew, what a captain! They left all of us floundering in their wake. Let them eat fully of our fare.

Bekederemo: The trouble is your women add too many condiments to their food, all in their one desire to enslave their husbands. Make sure they don't seduce my men.

Egbe: It's your sister doing the cooking, my good friend, not any Itsekiri witch.

Bekederemo: O, blame me now for giving you my sister against my father's wish. Now where is she? Fiobode, Fiobode, come back here and help me out of these clothes.

Egbe: With your outfit, you made us all beggars today. I could see the old man shaking all over.

Bekederemo: Let him shake some more. A man in government pay, he asked for a pageant for his master, didn't he? Now, help me out of this, if my sister won't do it.

Egbe: You know she went for your food.

Fiobode: No, here I am, I went to put away the coral beads, the gold chain -

Bekederemo: All right, and you forgot the food.

Egbe: Now, which one do you want first – to eat or to get out of your outfit?

Bekederemo: Both. Yes, I want food and I also want to get out of this gear or I shall take back my sister that I helped you elope with much to my father's anger.

Egbe: Oh no, no, I remain for ever in your debt, Osio. Several years after, your father still refused to bless the union even with the coming of Teye, a mermaid of a child fit to calm a crocodile.

Bekederemo: You should have produced him more children instead of being the lazy couple that you are. Now, bring me the food, Fiobode, before I change my mind.

Fiobode: It's right here, my brother, it's right here.

Bekederemo: First, help me out of these shoes. I should have brought in my men. But tell me, Egbe, is this how your wife looks after you, starves you all day?

Egbe: Not at all, not at all, she is a great girl, if anything she overfeeds me like a baby at her breast.

Bekederemo: There you are. You give her too much room. Look at it, you've even allowed her to build a compound of her own. Is she going to marry wives to fill it? I gave away a nanny, not a billy-goat.

Egbe: Osio! Ogodolile! Ikhimi! You and your mouth! There, I smell a pot of smoking *ukodo*. I wonder what manner of condiments she's loaded it with – Ijaw ones, I wager.

Bekederemo: Get away with you. You take over other people's things and make them your own. I regret sometimes I gave you my sister.

Egbe: Too late now. But come to think of it, I've always wondered what the old Ijaw girl from Kiagbodo did to Ofiagbere that he fell so deeply into her arms and never woke up again.

Bekederemo: I'm not taking your bait. It was the other way round. Igedi came, she fell, and she fled home with her secret not knowing she was carrying my mother Koko. So, Fiobode, you are here at last.

Fiobode: Yes, let me set down the dishes, my brother, who fills me with love.

Bekederemo: You keep your love for your husband. I have more than a load of it in my compound at Kiagbodo, and God knows it is tough work coping with it. Egbe, now I can feel the breeze blowing about me. When are you going to get out of your clothes? These dresses make masquerades of us, all for these receptions we have to hold for these people whenever they descend on us. First, they came merely to trade in oil, content to stay in their hulks offshore. Now they have come ashore, commanding us in one endless train like the guinea worm: District Officers or Commissioners, they call themselves, next Residents and High Commissioners, then Lt. Governors, and now it is not only a Governor, handing down laws, one day from Ibadan and from Enugu another day, but a man styled Governor-General and Commander-in-Chief, in Lagos, newly come down from somewhere called Kaduna or is it Zungeru up in Hausa land. A mere tortoise of a fellow – just this high. And it's not only oil they talk of these days for which, mind you, they fix all the prices, but plain possession and transfer of our land. Remember how Commissioner Crawford displaced the Ogbe people from this headland to build a trading post now called Warri. Oh, my brother, there is a strange disease now spreading among us that you and I do not know. The terrible thing is that it is our own man Dore helping them to spread it, first from Benin River and now to Warri River and all around, since Ayube mysteriously shot himself.

Egbe: It's not just Ijaw and Urhobo lands here that he is signing away without the peoples' knowledge and consent. He has done it at Okere, at Sapele, and now he is signing away more for a new place called Alder's Town, all in the name of our Olu that every child knows died before his grand parents were born. In return, the white man carves for the man a portion of the land that can hardly take the quarters for his cook and steward.

Fiobode: Please listen, my husband, my brother, I believe the man himself is shouting at the gate. (*A loud angry voice is heard outside shouting for Bekederemo and Egbe*).

Bekederemo: You can at least give it to him he is his father's son, the adventurer.

Egbe: Now, what brings him here?

Fiobode: Shall I serve later then. The man won't let you eat. He means trouble.

Bekederemo: He is welcome to share our meal. So much sweating he did today, running around in his oversized robes to impress his masters, he must be starving. But remember I eat my royal fish whole as rolled tail to mouth. No sharing.

Egbe: Osio, you are impossible! Now, don't rub pepper into his wounds raw as they are. We know he wants blood, but just leave him to me, and watch how I pour him oil.

Fiobode: I better go and cook some more food, if he'll be persuaded to eat

Bekederemo: Calm yourselves, you two. Egbe, where are your liveried household staff that my sister has to do everything by herself? The things you people pick up from the white man! Fancy dressing up in white drain-pipe trousers and tunics, all topped by toupee helmets. And all those brass buttons running all the way to their dog collars. Amazing they don't choke in their parades.

(Still shouting, Dore enters, pulled in on a rickshaw by a boy on a bicycle)

Dore: Bekederemo, Bekederemo, I know you are there celebrating with that brother-in-law of yours.

Bekederemo: *(walking away)* Should I be celebrating with strangers? Or with my enemies?

Egbe: *(going to meet Dore)* Welcome, my great leader, welcome! How do we deserve this visit? I thought you would be deep in conclave with our imperial visitors, discussing great matters of state.

Dore: There, get out of my way! Bekederemo, you disgraced me today, yes, - right in front of His Excellency the Governor - General, His Honour the Resident, His Worship the District Officer. Who made you head masquerade?

Bekederemo: I am just a poor trader in palm oil.

Egbe: It was a great show for everybody, my elder. One masquerade cannot make a festival.

Dore: Shame on you! I know you conspired with him to humiliate me today.

Egbe: God forbid! Truly, the gods and our ancestors know we did not.

Dore: Before all the imperial party present, not to mention the assemblage of all warrant chiefs drawn from Itsekiri, Ijo, Urhobo, Isoko...

Bekederemo: ...and Aboh and Kwale there present. Now, how did I manage to do that to the owner of all these lands?

Dore: Bekederemo, don't dare me! You are not my age mate. Holy Ibrikimo, by what spirit are you driven?

Egbe: Don't be angry great leader. Nobody disputes age with you. You are older than us by far.

Dore: You were there when he stole the show - from the regatta to the reception at the residency. It was upon him all eyes were turned like a bride in the market place, and His Excellency talked to him more than to me, his appointed political agent.

Egbe: Oh, he did not on purpose...

Dore: You saw it all, much to the laughter of the crowd watching the regatta, parade, and procession of Chiefs that he led without permission.

Bekederemo: I see; so that's the new crime that we've committed. If I had kept the rear, you would have said it was a deliberate build-up.

Dore: You can't dispute the fact that you bedecked your *okolada* with banners you specially imported from England, flew a dozen flags for a boat of thirty-two paddlers, all dressed up in red, green and purple, and you yourself wearing a beaded hat, robe of gold over silk wrapper and chain of beads and gold, flowing down your chest, and all round your arms more bands of coral beads, weren't you playing king to us all with your umbrella and staff fit for a crowned head?

Bekederemo: A regatta is supposed to be a festival. So you and Resident Douglas billed the occasion, and you specifically invited us to come in full, correct dress. In Hausaland, from which our great guest has just descended, you said it is called there the durbar - which brings out Sultan and all Emirs there in one, calvacade of riders on horses, challenging the rainbow.

Dore: You should have brought your ship, why didn't you bring your famous ship? That would have trumpeted your message to the entire world.

Egbe and Fiobode: (*together*) He didn't mean to disgrace you! Your canoe too was a great spectacle. He meant no harm at all!

Dore: Oh, yes, he didn't mean to humiliate me before the white man. But you saw how all the other chiefs waded into the waters as one team to carry him shoulder-high to land, as if he were the Governor himself whose feet must not touch water and mud. Tabuko of Oguname, Uba of Ubogo, Okarusi of Ughelli, Buluku of Oteri, Adamagu of Keremor, Ogboru of Abraka - shall I name many more who forgot their own dignity and fineries, many of them, I swear, borrowed, who rushed into those muddy waters of our beach? I shall deal with all of them later, make them sit in sun and rain on the veranda of my court, if I don't jail them outright.

Bekederemo: Please turn your anger on me, and leave our neighbours out of it.

Dore: Bekederemo, don't dare me further. Do you hear me, don't dare me. Nana tried it, and you saw what happened to him. The proud merchant prince, as he called himself, came back from Accra to Koko, a mere carpenter. I hear he is now your great customer for gunpowder. The man doesn't listen. And as for the mighty Oba of Benin, need I remind you he never returned home from his Calabar captivity? There he still lies today, in a plot, built over by a common Urhobo man.

Bekederemo: Don't you threaten me! There you are, you have an elephant slung over your shoulder, and you are still digging the earth for crickets with your toe.

Dore: The hippopotamus looks for a canoe, it also wants a paddle.

Bekederemo: And when the hippopotamus spits, it is its own head it spits on.

Dore: Oh, is that so? Well, we'll see. We know you have your cannons, your armoury right behind your kiln, and barrels and barrels of gun powder passing as palm oil.

Bekederemo: File whatever reports you like to your masters. I am not Nana nor the unfortunate king of Benin. I came into the world in my own canoe, and I didn't come to take other peoples' land.

Dore: Oh, yes, you came to trade, and a great market you've made of it with the white man you distrust so much - Ijaw man that you are. A pirate people, you wait and see, the white man will contain you as he has better people on land.

Bekederemo: Will you also pilot them to your grandmother's town Isaba?

Egbe: Enough, please, enough, I beg both of you, my leader and my brother! Let's not kill ourselves on account of this stranger in our midst. Oh may God not let us.

Dore: He calls himself Rain that puts out Fire, the Shroud that covers the Dead, The Man who only has to speak and his will is done, all these and cther extravagant appellations he bestows on himself. Better warn your brother-in-law to stay in his village of Kiagbodo before he comes embarrassing me another time in Warri.

Bekederemo: Your village, Odogene, I thought, is the village of all villages. And you know the real owners of Warri.

Dore: Did you hear that, Egbe, did you hear your brother-in-law? Next, he will say Ode Itsekiri is a hamlet.

Egbe: He certainly will not. Who upholds his right hand so high that he would deny his own left hand?

Fiobode: I am on my knees, our great leader! Oh, what could have caused this storm on such a sunny day like this! Some witches of Ugbawangwe must be at work again in broad daylight. Night and day should not collide.

Dore: I tell you. Bekederemo disgraced me today before the whole world. The only thing he didn't do today is proclaim himself king.

Bekederemo: Far from it. All our flags flew under your overarching one, proclaiming you "Honourable Paramount Chief, Olu of Itsekiri, Urhobo, Ijaws, Warri." The little we did really passed as the handle to hold up your splendid umbrella.

Dore: Was that what they wrote on my flag? How was I to know it? You know our boys write what they like about us to promote themselves, knowing you and I cannot read.

Bekederemo: Yes, we all know clerk, interpreter, and even the messenger, have a language of their own that creates problems between us and the white man. So we shall not blame you for the claims made in your name.

Dore: Look at him! When he wants to, he can be winning in his ways, melting you down like the palm oil that brings him his riches. But most of the time, true to his praise names, he fears nobody. Now, don't you defend him anymore; he left you to rot for this in a cell. You knew how rats nibbled at the soles of your feet so that when I let you out, you walked as if the courtyard was spilled with kernel shells. And remember how your face and chest became a field for mosquitoes, no, cockroaches to dance on all through the night so that you wished you had a hundred hands to beat them off. All because the richest man in all our rivers would not pay a simple fine. Why the Resident let him go I still cannot understand.

Bekederemo: I refused to pay the fine because it was unjust. I fought your father-in-law in a fair duel, presided over by our Pere Osiota. Your father-in-law even boasted you were coming to watch the event. The man almost murdered me when against all rules of the game, he failed to stop his men from hurling their cudgels at me when I lost my wrapper rolled about my head. But since God does not sleep, it took my sister Ekpughele to restore my gear while all my men fell back. She lost all her teeth in the act. And when finally I drove your father-in-law off the field and would have pursued him to his doorstep but for the intervention of the king, the man runs to you for revenge.

Dore: Well, you paid in the end, anyway.

Bekederemo: If you must know, it was my aunts who paid your fine on account of their daughter who would not stop wailing for her man in prison.

Egbe: Yes, yes, so it was. I was quite all right.

Dore: (*mimicking Egbe*) Yes, I was quite all right! What charm have these people put on you! You are so besotted with his sister you spent days in His Majesty's cell, while the greatest merchant of all our rivers refused to pay a simple fine levied by a properly constituted court of law.

Egbe: Great leader, it was merely his way of protesting what everybody thought too high a fine in the alleged offence.

Dore: Egbe! How dare you defend the man still after what he did to you?

Bekederemo: Admit it, my elder, have you ever seen a thousand English pounds in your life, although you work for the British?

Dore: There, Egbe, you see him insulting me right in front of you?

Egbe: Not so, not so, great leader.

Dore: Not so, not so, great leader. Truly, they have given you charms to eat.

Bekederemo: My sister carries no charms in amulets, only her natural gifts that enable the weakest woman carry her man, even like the delicate dish she serves him.

Dore: Hear the hawk playing the morning-bird!

Bekederemo: The hawk does not live for the chicken.

Dore: Why must you always swoop with every word spoken? I didn't call my daughter a witch.

Egbe: No, my elder, you did not. We all belong to Ogogomaro and therefore should not harm one another. As it is, we were just about to eat when you came in. That tells the good things you wish in your heart for this household. So let's have your prayers.

Fiobode: That's right! Be good to us and dip your fingers in our humble dish.

Dore: Humble dish you call that! All right, let us sit down and eat. It has been a long day. Fiobode, did you cook yourself? The aroma is all over the house. Now, where are your famous liveried staff to serve us our good Gordon gin?

Bekederemo: I too have asked for their service but they all seem to have got too much soup on their white tunics and trousers to show up for service.

Egbe: As a matter of fact, if you really want to know, several were drafted to service today at the Residency. But no matter. What greater privilege is there for me than to get my leader the fine bottle myself? Now, Fiobode, quick, quick, with the food so our great leader can bless it.

Dore: Yes, let's go and taste what the Ijo girl has to offer -
Bekederemo: of her Itsekiri skills.

Dore: Oh, yes, yes. We know you Oshoron descendants. Since our Akengbuwa Olus died within a week of each other, father and son, you have been out of a job. No head to carry off at the king's demise. Amazing, wasn't it? For son to present his father with a strand of his grey hair on a plate and the old man sending him in return a gift of a bottle of honey. As for me, let's eat now - the heart and lungs for me. Someone already has a heart too big for his chest. The head of the cow I shall carry home to Odogene. Don't forget I want to take the tide back. We don't have a ship like some people.
(Fiobode leads the men in to eat.)

II

School report

At Kiagbodo, inside Bekederemo's main house at the far end of the compound. As part of the general hubbub normal to the place, a boy can be heard crying out for help in the courtyard with his mother urging on the man administering punishment on her truant son.

Bekederemo: (*seated in his favourite swivel chair*) Is Branuvwere there?

Branuvwere: Here I am, Osio, son of Odogbolomo, Agbalakirigbagba –

Bekederemo: That'll do, Branuvwere, that will do for now. Tell Fuludu to stop the punishment.

Branuvwere: Immediately, at once; your wish shall be done, Osioname, Ogodolile, Ikperinvwin Ajigbila –

Bekederemo: The boy is taking more beating while you are pouring on me praise names. I did not go to school before I made my fortune.

Branuvwere: That's true, that's true, child of God's favourite, I go right away. But father and son, communicating without speech, here comes Fuludu himself.

Fuludu: We've finished, father. I fear that boy won't be able to use his buttocks for some days.

Bekederemo: Let's hope he learns the lesson he ran away from at school.

Fuludu: There it is sons of slaves that the white man has brought back with him who do the drubbing.

Bekederemo: And with a vengeance that we all understand. When Sir Ralph Moor at Bonny first asked us chiefs of the Niger Delta to send our sons to the new schools they were setting up, from Ogungunmanga to Sapele, as part and instrument of their administration, you will all recall I had my doubts. Nor did the Yoruba man Ajayi Crowther who came as a priest of their God convince many of us. I made my money as did my father, when he wasn't warring even with his father's people, without the help of the white man and his education.

Branuvwere: True, true. That was Ogein my master, son of Ndorowei and Bado; he would leap out of his full laden boat to take on a crocodile mid-river.

Fuludu: They set up no schools in my time, not to talk of your age.

Bekederemo: But adults we know answered their bells that call them everyday to gather in one place to learn and pray. Your own brother Okemeji learnt to read and write, as a grown up man.

Branuvwere: And you had already married him three wives. Osio, it is you who spoil the boys. Each with a house of his own and wives to match. And all of them fed all day by their father who does not forget sisters and brothers.

Bekederemo: Stop it now, Branuvwere. All riches come from God.

Branuvwere: Not to give away. Men with wives and children of their own, not only eating at their mothers, but forever raiding your common kitchen, open night and day. How will these children learn to look after themselves.

Fuludu: Some of us have begun in our own little way.

Bekederemo: Yes, how is the trade at Patani and Asabase?

Fuludu: As down here the white man dictates the price of oil and…

Bekederemo: Yes, a curious market they have established for themselves, a buyer dictating to the seller the price of his goods.

Branuvwere: *Ikperinvwin*, Man of your words, you have not lost by the arrangement.

Bekederemo: Well, so they say, so it seems. But the accounts get more and more difficult to keep in the head or count on the fingers. Can you calculate the sum of a hundred and one casks of oil, five hundred odd bags of kernel or a hold of bags of salt or of bales of cloth all in your head? The white man does it all with his ready reckoner while he is pouring you a glass of J.J. W. Peters. That's why some of us agreed to send our children to school. Not all of them; just a few to test the waters. You know others, like Nana, even after his troubles and return home, chose to send children of their slaves to the white man to do what he liked with them. I sent Orumala, James and Ajaluwa to the new Government School in Warri. Egbe, my friend and brother, also sent his one son Asifo. He survived, bore the beating at the hands of slaves, set free by the white man who bought them in the first instance, and in his scheme of things has returned them to us to teach us his ways, and now they punish us as coopers, produce examiners, store-keepers and beach masters.

Branuvwere: Some of us never left these shores -

Bekederemo: Well, with the House Rule Ordinance, proclaimed by that man Lugard, all slaves are now free to go. It says something that Ejobone, Efemini, Ogagoma, Rakatene, Ecama and scores of others choose to stay with us. But see how Dakaraba, Okonkwo and their gang ran out like chicken after corn, whether in their new found freedom or for the 12 pounds set on each head, I still can not tell.

Branuvwere: Well, here I stay and here I shall die, as I have lived with your father and now with you. Indeed, where will I go if I even wanted to? My one prayer left in life is to be born into the family of Ogein and Bekederemo when I come back again to this world.

Bekederemo: Is it such a sweet time here in this world that you want to come back again when you die, Branuvwere! But have it as you please. You have been like an uncle and elder brother to me in my father's house of raging material always on the edge of catching fire.

Branuvwere: I will never forget when the women of the royal house of Ogiogio descended on the place with torches and firebrands all determined to burn it down, because you had eloped with their daughter, a regular princess. Fuludu, that's how you were first called Wareyonmo. House burner, that's what you were.

Fuludu: Yes, Branuvwere, I've been told that story so many times that I shall grow deaf like the iguana lizard.

Branuvwere: That's correct. Renaming you Velvet has not softened father and son in any way.

Bekederemo: Enough of deeds done and not done in days gone by. Let's think of now and the times ahead, Branuvwere. You go and give the boy a packet of biscuits and a tin of corned beef or sardine if that's what he wants.

Branuvwere: That's how you spoil them - rewarding the wayward. What will the good and the obedient do?

Bekederemo: Just go and give the boy something to soothe his sores. And if you like, you may as well break a case of biscuits and another of canned fish or meat for all the children to share, if that will bring peace.

Branuvwere: And the women and the men?

Bekederemo: As you like - and before you pile up more servants and slaves, make sure Tabeta knows what you do with his store.

Branuvwere: You see what I said -

Bekederemo: Go, man, go!

Branuvwere: Oh, Osioname, Ogodolile, Iron that is steel, One who says and does it. I've got fresh energy in my old bones. (*He ambles out*)

Fuludu: Now, may I go also?

Bekederemo: Not to join in the play for women and children. Now, how's that boy Clark? Strange I've already forgotten the Itsekiri name I gave him.

Fuludu: It is well, for so it was prescribed by priest, doctor and oracle.

Bekederemo: Yes, yes, I remember. So how is the boy doing at Patani?

Fuludu: That was one thing I was going to report to you since my arrival home.

Bekederemo: Don't tell me he's had another accident.

Fuludu: Not quite so. But one day before I came home from a trip to Ndoni and Aboh, that man Afentu Oki had conspired with Umukoko to send off my son to Ashaka in Kwale to school.

Bekederemo: So he is with his aunt Orughurugha and her husband Robert Milne?

Fuludu: Yes, father. I beat the woman almost to death, and as for that man Oki with whom she has Isoko connection, I have banned him from my compound.

Bekederemo: But I thought he's your landlord and best friend.

Fuludu: I banned him all the same before he converts my entire household to his new religion. When I get back to station, I intend to collect my son.

Bekederemo: No, my son, you will leave my grandson at school. I was already thinking of sending him to Mr. Bruce at Burutu.

Fuludu: But –

Bekederemo: I have spoken. This is a boy you almost lost once in a storm at the point the Forcados River and the River Nun join hands. Now he's on solid land in the hands of his aunt and her husband, leave my son there to learn the ways of the white man. If yam does not grow through its head, it will through its tail-end. I did not change his name to Clark for laughter.

Fuludu: I know his aunt is your favourite daughter, but everybody knows she is as strict as an Itsekiri matron. They beat and starve their wards like slaves all in the name of discipline.

Bekederemo: A little discipline will do him good. Better still, as I said, he'll learn the ways of the white man where all his uncles have failed. It is a matter of great pride for my friend Egbe, his son Asifo is today on his way to Sierra Leone en-route to England to study law. Who knows the future?

Fuludu: If you say so, father.

Bekederemo: Yes, I do. Now call me Piniki. He should be back by now from Erhuwanren. I wonder how my friend Okajivor is coping with the court the British have set up there. (*Fuludu leaves*)

Bekederemo: (*breaking into song*)

> Now, it is thrown wide open
> Now it is thrown wide open
> Wide, wide open
> All you who go to the white man

> All you who speak his tongue
> Now it is thrown wide open
> Wide, wide open
>
> Don't you go behind backbiting
> Now it's thrown wide open
> Wide, wide open
>
> It is now between you and me
> Yes, its now between you and me
> Now all is thrown wide open
> Wide, wide open!

Bekederemo: (*to Piniki, his bard, who has tiptoed in and has been listening all the time*) How about that, Piniki for a new number, how about that for verse and refrain?

Piniki: Very strong clear beat, Sir, very easy to pick up. The call is clear and the chorus flows direct from it.

Bekederemo: Do you think so, Piniki? You Ujevwen bards lick one round while skinning him to the bone like a shark.

Piniki: Not so, Sir, not so, I really mean it. The lines are clear-cut, the beat strong. It lends itself straight to dance.

Bekederemo: Then let's try it, shall we?

Piniki: Of course, Sir, of course, but you know, as for body movement, you set the pace for us to follow hands and feet.

Bekederemo: Flatterer, flatterer, as some compose so others dance. (*They sing and dance together, he remaining seated*) And if you think it's worth adding to our repertoire, let's take it to them outside. (*Both go out, singing the new song, and many can be heard joining and cheering in the great square of the compound*).

III

Court returns

At Warri, in the Provincial Court of Appeal, at close of sitting.

Dore: (*presiding*) Now, where were we before that idiot interpreter rudely interrupted us?

Court Clerk Bar Rolle: Eleven goats, eight male, three female -

Dore: The female are a better catch. That I've always told you, for they will breed and breed while the male, with horns and balls, forever disputing ascendancy, are good only for sacrifice. I want more females.

Court Clerk: Yes, Chief. I won't forget next time.

Dore: What about chickens?

Court Clerk: Two dozen hatches, Sir, most of them female.

Dore: How many exactly?

Court Clerk: That the messenger is sorting out right now.

Dore: And eggs? Don't tell me they are all non-layers.

Court Clerk: Yes, Sir, There are more than six baskets of eggs, mainly from the Abraka case.

Dore: Good. Those people will never stop coming to court. Indeed, the Sobo as a whole, love going to court on any and every matter. A man steps over the outstretched legs of a woman, it is to them adultery. They come to you for land to farm today; tomorrow they are in court claiming it as inheritance from their father. Oh, they will even take an appeal on a case that they have won. A more litigious group you'll never find anywhere. That's why we recommended Native Courts at places like Abraka, Okpare, Frukama, Erhuwanren and such other places. Incidentally, what returns did Shangbe make today at Okpare?

Court Clerk: No reports yet, Chief, except to say that Bekederemo broke up a session.

Dore: Not again! When was this? That's how he scatters the court at Frukama, I hope Osadjere did not join him. He gave a girl in marriage to the man. I must have the whole report at once on this matter.

Court Clerk: Yes, Sir.

Dore: Meanwhile in the matter of the chickens and eggs, you know very well what to do.

Court Clerk: Yes of course, Chief. The District Officer must have his eggs for breakfast every morning with his bread and tea. We've made adequate arrangement.

Dore: Anything to wash down these items? We want no bone sticking in our throat.

Court Clerk: The Ijaw cases took good care of that, Chief. Jars and demijohns of gin enough to fill a cask. They are being stacked up in rows right now.

Dore: Make sure seven at least are taken to my boat. The gods at home are dry right now. Not to mention my ancestors. It's a bull our late Olu really wants. But what are we to do? The people are getting wiser every day, thanks to agitators like Bekederemo. His people at Ayakoroma used to bring me bundles of *aloku* poles to provide me with beautiful rafters for my compound without asking questions. Now it takes the threat of a hot warrant of arrest to make them behave, I have to deal with them.

Messenger: Great Paramount Chief of Itsekiri, Sobo –

Dore: Go straight to your message, you rascal from Batere.

Messenger: Well, Sir, I throw away my salute. I just want to report a big delegation is out there to see you. So troublesome are they I had to leave off the stock I was taking.

Dore: Who are they? Let them sit on the ground outside. Don't you see we are busy making returns for the day?

Messenger: I can see it with my own eyes, my Paramount Chief.

Dore: I'm sure they are Sobo – not from Agbassa, I hope. I have just taken new parcels of land from them without their knowledge and consent. The white man seems to need more land every day, not just for his stores, I see, but for offices, barracks and quarters for his supporting staff from Sierra Leone and Gold Coast. Well, I say, let them wait outside in the sun.

Messenger: I don't think they are Sobos, Sir.

Dore: Whoever they are, go and tell them the white man doesn't like a noise anywhere near him. They even want to stop us drumming at night at Ode Itsekiri.

Court Clerk: Thank God the G.R.A is quite some distance away.

Dore: A good distance away? If the wind does not carry it all the way, some people who don't like us will go and report our Court of Appeal has become Ogbe Ijo market. (*The noise comes nearer*)

Dore: Messenger, go tell them I shall order all of them arrested and sent to the deaf house. It could be the Isoko are here again with another murder case. Those people from Oleh and Usere, they are so free with their cutlasses we must recommend for them an expedition.

Messenger: If I may tell the bitter truth, Sir, my Chief, I think they are Ijo people.

Dore: Izon people –?

Messenger: Yes, Sir, Paramount Chief, from Kiagbodo, I believe, for I think it is your wife's people I saw there weeping.

Dore: (*rising in fury*) My own wife – Ditimi?

Messenger: Yes, my great Chief, so they said.

Court Clerk: I don't believe it. What could have happened? That is the home of the great Bekederemo himself.

Dore: Shut your big mouth there, will you, before I slap it shut for you permanently. I don't know, you returned slaves from abroad, you never know your limits in service of the white man. Messenger, go bring in my in-laws, no, not the whole crowd as you described, just the leader of the group, for a man of worth must have led them here from my father-in-law.

(*The Messenger rushes out and returns almost immediately with a man looking very aggrieved.*)

What is this, Babigha, is it you yourself, my dear father-in-law? Now, can't you speak man? It must be that man Bekederemo again. Did he touch my mermaid wife Ditimi on her breasts, her buttocks? That man knows no bounds, but this time, surely, he has broken all barriers. Oh, Brikimo, protect us! Bar Rolle, our Court Clerk, do you see it was my wife's father that they left out there in the sun like a common Sobo complainant all this time?

Babigha: Yes, it's me but it is not about your wife that I have come.

Court Clerk: I would have been surprised if in the middle of the fight a man had the eye for a woman.

Dore: That's where you are so like a child. A condition of disorder like that is the best to do the most illegal acts. Everybody knows the British made away with the wealth of Benin when they took that city. And they did not spare any beautiful woman they ran into in the street. Why, look at what they did to our own stubborn kin before that. Forget every other item. I was there on both occasions, as you know. They found a thousand bottles of gin in Nana's stock. These they promptly carted away. How else do you think they keep their lonely hours in the bush? In company of our girls, bottle in one hand, and a revolver in the other. That is how they keep peace in these parts. I admit that. And the man Bekederemo has an appetite for acquisition as great as any of them. That's why they are such good business partners together. He chose trade, I politics. Indeed, one follows the other, they say. Look at the man. He is rumoured to have some seventy wives, and he still cannot keep his hands off the one wife a man has in his town.

Babigha: He poured on me excrement.

Messenger: Sorry, Sir, I didn't recognize the old man at first. With all his welts and bruises, he looked as if a sergeant-major had given him 36 lashes with *koboko*.

Dore: Babigha, don't tell me Bekederemo did this to you - you the son of Ogede, Arbiter for all your nine clans before the white man came to our rivers. And where was your king Pere Osiota and his council of chiefs while all this was happening?

Babigha: The man with his wealth has all of them in his pocket. Oh! the shame of my life, the man not only had me whipped but actually strung me up in the open market place, after burning down my people's shrine. And right now, he has many of my men in stocks for you to come and rescue. He said you may come again to Kiagbodo if you dare, being my son in-law.

Dore: This is too much. I want the man brought before me.

Court Clerk: Yes, Chief, I thoroughly concur.

Babigha: I'm the age mate of Ogein, his father, and he did this to me, because he has behind him the Niger Company.

Dore: Somebody call me Mr. Paul quick or Mr. Bucknor, if he's not there. This story must be told in the presence of a lawyer. I'm sure he is out there among suspects seeking bail. (*He paces up and down; goes up to Babigha to inspect closely his bruises and welts.*) And you people say I am the tyrant the white man has installed in a kingdom that never was.

Mr. Bucknor: What is this I see, Chief? Has there been a riot again among the natives?

Dore: Now tell your story for the lawyer to hear.

Babigha: It is the old dispute over the pantheon of gods at our town gate, set up by my son, Fetaroro. They are arbiter gods, especially the central one, Okpokpaye, famous for settling disputes in Kiagbodo and districts all around. But Bekederemo claims Madam, that's her name, is a killer, that whole families, wards, and entire districts have been wiped out by her. Now, yesterday he called in Mr. Grant, the District Officer, from Forcados, and under his cover, he burnt down our shrine.

Dore: Mr. Bucknor, the white man gave us freedom to worship in our old ways, didn't he?

Mr. Bucknor: Yes, Chief, he did; there is absolute freedom of worship, excepting of course the practice of any religion that calls for human sacrifice and cannibalism in the name of some fetish god.

Dore: So what shall we do with the man? This time he surely has entered our trap, and he will have to cut his limb into two to get out of it.

Court Clerk: Did I hear him say the Assistant District Officer at Forcados supervised the operation?

Mr. Bucknor : Yes, that was what I too heard. We have to go carefully into the case. There is a prohibition of the trial of Chiefs in either the Supreme or Native Courts; that is the new order by Sir Frederick Lugard.

Dore: My father-in-law is humiliated before his family, the protective goddess of his people burnt to ashes at the behest of Bekederemo in a most cleverly contrived operation, carried out in broad day light, and you are citing some law unknown to me. We have burnt down settlements for less than this in the time of Moor and Moorhouse.

Messenger: Yes, I remember –

Dore: Shut up your mouth, you fat head. I did not ask you to speak. Mr. Bucknor, what shall we do with the man? I want him brought before me under warrant of arrest. Even a Warrant Chief can issue one, and am I not Paramount Chief and President of the Native Court of Appeal?

Bucknor: Yes, no disputing that, Chief, but such a warrant of arrest can only be applied for and issued in serious charges such as murder, dangerous wounding, burglary -

Court Clerk: Furthermore, you will recall, Mr. Bucknor, as District Officer Maddocks illustrated, here it is in the aforesaid memo; "In some cases a man gets his enemy locked up on a false charge simply with the intention of stealing his goods, appropriating his woman…"

Dore: Oh, holy Brikimo! Bring me Bekederemo!

Bucknor: The Chief lives in another division. So service and execution of a criminal summons will require the endorsement of the District Officer at Forcados.

Dore: I am called Paramount Ruler, and yet can't thumb mark a warrant of arrest for that man?

Mr. Bucknor: Not so, Chief, if you will listen to what I have to say at this juncture, for surely the supervising officer at the scene must have made his report already to headquarters, so that I am sure the Resident has the file in his hand at this very moment that we are talking. What I would like to suggest, subject to your approval, Chief, is a simple direct approach to the matter, not recourse to the law courts, at least not at this stage, for that, you know, Chief, he has the money to drag on the case for as long as he likes, even for years, especially if it turns out to be a criminal matter as it appears to be.

Dore: All right, what will you have me do to save me from this disgrace, Mr. Bucknor? I can't follow all your grammar.

Mr. Bucknor: Let Babigha, I believe I pronounce the name correctly, let him, his daughter and his group retire home—

Dore: And I do nothing?

Mr. Bucknor: No. Sir, they will all come back to town, preferably with a larger crowd. Let them all at that time throw themselves on the ground, roll many times in the mud, and if possible, rub all over their bodies from head to toe the ashes from their god that he burnt down, and then let them pour back into town in all their numbers, straight to the provincial office, and there, raising their voices all to one man, even like women, cry for justice for the great wrong done them in full view of His Majesty's Government.

Dore: Brilliant, brilliant, Mr. Bucknor. Now, are you from Sierra Leone or Jamaica? I'll give you one of our girls to marry, that is, if your missus will not invoke upon her poor head the law of the God you follow.

Mr. Bucknor: Oh, Chief, oh, Chief, don't you worry about that. I believe we can arrange it. Yes, we can manage it, all right.

Dore: Then Court dismissed.

Messenger: We closed a long time ago, Chief.

Court Clerk: Fool, you'll get yourself locked up one of these days and nobody will bail you.

Dore: Not just that. We shall make him captain of the gang from Okere High College to go mow the elephant grass threatening our compound.

IV

Envoys

A chamber in Bekederemo's main house at Kiagbodo, a punkah fan swirling overhead from the ceiling.

Branuvwere: With a workload like this on my head in one day, I shall be buried alive before my time.

Nemugha: Hear, hear! All you have done today is get in the way of delegates, because you want to announce everybody.

Bekederemo: Don't mind the man. He has outlived my father and still looks like he could outlive me with his endless attention. Now, go and see our guests are well looked after.

Branuvwere: Of course, of course, I hope they have not broken some of our priceless dishes. You could see some of them eating with both hands as if the white man had put them away for days in his deaf house. Now they are there in the house you built for your company visitors, all of them, many from their mud and thatch homes, eating today in an iron and glass house, brought all the way from England. What if they break the windows or carry away some precious silver ware under their clothes? Bekederemo, your generosity will wreck you one day.

Nemugha: Your tongue outruns your thoughts, old man. Remember the power of the word.

Branuvwere: What have I said that you his adviser should not tell him in all truth? All you people do now is talk and drink.

Nemugha: Know yourself, Branuvwere!

Bekederemo: You know him well. Branuvwere, our guests may be making away by now with some of your heirloom while you stand here talking.

Branuvwere: That's true, that's true! (*He scampers out almost stumbling into Fuludu who is coming in*).

Bekederemo: Yes?

Fuludu: Another delegation has just arrived.

Nemugha: Another one? Where from? The Urhobo from Abraka to Olomu; the Isoko from Iyede to Oweh, the Ijaw from Ekeremor to Ayakoroma; the Aboh and Kwale, all have come with their accounts of the damages done to them by this wild elephant that the white man has let loose on us. Accounts of palm oil produce extorted with little or no pay, demands for the best timber for rafters for his house, forced labour to build roads, illegal arrests of men so he can take over their wives, seizure of young girls to breach their virginity for public display, capture of other peoples' livestock to make sacrifice to his gods and ancestors, dispossession of people of their God-given land – oh, what a flash flood now sweeps over our land! Who is left that does not suffer in this province?

Fuludu: This is a delegation of Itsekiri people.

Nemugha: From the Itsekiri? But these are the beneficiaries of this strange harpooning together of disparate peoples by the white man in his new order.

Bekederemo: You may not know it, but Dogho's kin and people also suffer a lot at his hand, perhaps more so than others. For instance, he has proclaimed himself Olu of Itsekiri, a throne that has been vacant for generations. In that spirit he makes sacrifices of bullocks at Odogene to his ancestors contrary to the customs of the people.

Nemugha: Your mother's people do have some strange traditions.

Bekederemo: Fuludu, who do they say they represent?

Fuludu: They come directly from Nana.

Bekederemo and Nemugha: (*together*) From Nana? No!

Fuludu: Yes, they say they are from Nana himself, and I know Johnson, his son, who leads them. I overheard them say a certain William Moore is also on his way with his team.

Bekederemo: Now the broth thickens. Let them in. (*Fuludu goes out*). My elder, we must see the hunt to the end.

Nemugha: Of course, the child who says the mother should not sleep will find no sleep himself. This buffalo has walked over all farms.

(*Fuludu returns with Johnson Nana, voices of other members of his delegation close behind him*).

Johnson Nana (*kneeling*): Osioname! Ikperivwin! Ogodolile! my father sends you greetings and the prayers of an old man.

Bekederemo: Rise, my son, rise, son of Opubeni. Your father was indeed a great tide that swept up all our rivers. How is his health? I hope it is good. I have not been able to go and see him since his return home.

Johnson: The years, the trials have taken their toll.

Bekederemo: Come and sit by me, here, that's right, I want to hear at once what the old warrior has to say.

Johnson: My father, in the light of what is happening under this new regime, especially after the proclamation of the Home Rule Repeal Ordinance, is most concerned about what will happen to the Itsekiri race.

Bekederemo: Go on, my son.

Johnson: With all due respect and trepidation, Sir, let me say my father would rather I speak with you alone and in private.

Bekederemo: This is my guide and mentor since my unruly youth -

Nemugha: No, no, Osio, I'll go. It's time I stretched my old waist and knees. How you sit out meeting after meeting in the course of one day, I can't begin to understand.

Bekederemo: We'll do better than that. You stay where you are. Young man, come with me. Let's go into another room and hear your message.

(*He takes Johnson by the hand and goes into an inner room.*)

V

Chains

Before Bekederemo's great hall overlooking his beach at Kiagbodo. (Branuvwere and Piniki are sharing a joke.)

Mitovwodo: (*coming ashore with paddle in hand*) What is happening here again? I could hear the noise all the way to Ogboro. What am I saying? The noise came all the way to Oyiboba and quite distracted our oil workers.

Branuvwere: Mother of all children, you who match a whole city, you missed a great show.

Piniki: Oh, farm of cassava, you who alone are the starch, you who alone are the garri that we feed on, you really should have been here to see it. I saw it all.

Mitovwodo: Now, between the owl and the canary, who will let me hear the great news.

Branuvwere: Piniki is a small boy. So let me speak.

Piniki: No, I will tell the story. Age has no title to this. I saw it all; came ahead of the news in fact.

Mitovwodo: You flew ahead of the news - before it all happened? Now you poets!

Piniki: It is God's own truth, and it all began at Erhuwanren. Chief had sent me home to my uncle Chief Okajivo. Even as I arrived, a great panic broke across town. Why, what is happening, everybody was asking everybody. But the answer was there before everybody to see. A column of soldiers, Ma, not just cudgel - carrying policemen in black khaki, but real regular soldiers in red and green, Hausa or Godogodo men by their height, all armed with rifles slung over their shoulders, and behind them a group of porters with all manners of boxes on their heads. Madam, everyone knew then that it was not the usual court session about to open.

Mitovwodo: So what was it?

Piniki: My voice fails me.

Branuvwere: There, let me speak but you wouldn't agree.

Piniki: But you were not there, old man, I saw it all. Yes, close behind the porters, with another column of soldiers pulling at cannons and other heavy artillery guns after them, was a posse of white men, already dismounted from their bicycles, marching into town where no offence against government had been committed. It was a sight that made everybody wet their dresses. Men ran out to see only to run back with the women, seeing what they saw, and children, not already shooed in like chickens, hid between their mothers legs, almost causing their wrappers to fall from their waists.

Mitovwodo: Certainly, that couldn't have been the first time your people were seeing the white man in a show of force?

Branuvwere: Admit it, Ma, one albino, like our friend here, is quite enough sight. But to see a whole group of such men, all at once in one place, it is a scene fit to scare a hunting dog.

Piniki: God gave us our stamp, not man as with some people.

Mitovwodo: Now, now –

Piniki: We weren't seeing the white man display for the first time. These were different, fierce, several in number, all in military uniform and bush kit. "Where is the chief of this place?" a sergeant, yes, three stripes the man had on his sleeves, as bold as the Ibadan marks on his face, a bugle in his hand, "Where is the chief of this place?" he bellowed again. So they were shown to uncle's compound. He was already seated there in council, waiting for the worst. But will the white men sit down when he met them? No! They insisted on marching straight to the court house where they promptly billeted themselves in the rest house, ordering uncle to follow them there immediately, that their business was not with him, but that they wanted him to help, all the same, failing which he would have great cause to regret his refusal to co-operate.

Mitovwodo: Oh, these white people!

Piniki: Now, how did the secret of their mission come out?

Branuvwere: Go on with the story, and cut out the magic of poetry as you call it.

Mitovwodo: Yes, Piniki, go on; I am all ears.

Piniki: It was Enyevwiara, one of uncle's wives, who heard it drop, so to speak, out of the mouth of the porter. Soldiers had taken over the compound, you'll understand, Madam, and together with the porters, they were beginning to treat the place and everybody in it as their goods and chattel. But God is great! These invaders, intruders were only human beings after all, for so exhausted were they from the overland march from Warri, one dropped his box in trying to set it down. Guess what fell out, mother of all children.

Mitovwodo: No; what God has not created the white man is always trying to make. So tell me.

Piniki: Chains, this time. Chains, Madam, crude and raw, with padlocks attached, and of such weight it took a corporal to help the porter drag them back into the box with much clanging of iron, but not before giving him a round cuff on the head with the butt of his gun. "Oh, leave me alone," the poor porter cried. "Reserve your fire for Chief Bekederemo."

Mitovwodo: (*dropping her paddle*) So, have they taken him - all that noise that reached me at Oyiboba, was it the arrest of my husband? Oh, God will deal with that man Dore! Now, where have they taken him?

(*Both men restrain her as she tries to rush to the compound beyond*).

Branuvwere: Nowhere, nowhere, mother of children. Master is Osokpadamudiri, an immovable block of iron, who can pull him from the seat God gave him from birth? He is there right now in his Rest House, entertaining the white men. I wouldn't go and break up the party.

Mitovwodo: Yes, yes! You are right. Oh, my husband, husband of my youth! But I saw no gun-boat anchored on the main river, as I came back from Oyiboba.

Piniki: It happened like this. The expedition party came stealthily by land through Ogbodugbo, having ordered my uncle to ferry them there on peril of deportation. But like the black-kite, I was ahead of them already, sent by uncle to warn his friend.

Mitovwodo: Oh, God be praised, oh, Tamarasan, Altar of God, may evil forces never come through our gates!

Branuvwere and Piniki: (*together*) Ise! Ise! Ise!

Piniki: Chief is truly the son of God's favourite. How else can one account for this miracle? The party marched with such speed, they surprised me as I was delivering my message.

Branuvwere: Poetry is your gift, not athletic prowess. But the thing really was a miracle. Bekederemo was reclining there on that half wall of the hall, as he often does, when the enemy descended upon him, their commanding officer at the head. "Are you Chief Bekederemo?" he barked. "Yes, I am,!" Chief replied. "We have come to arrest you in the matter of the people's shrine that you burnt down." "Then you should first hear my side of the story", the Chief said. And all that patrol team of soldiers, porters and the white men with their guns, followed him into his compound like a ship its pilot.

Mitovwodo: Oh Piniki, I thank you, I thank you and your uncle. This time you ran like an antelope ahead of the leopard. I am no prophetess, although people call me names. But one day, the great friendship between our houses will be sealed by marriage of our children that will make us proud.

Piniki and Branuvwere: (*together again*) Ise! Ise! May it be so! And let it be so in my lifetime.

Piniki: Oh, at this great age of yours?

Mitovwodo: Why not, who knows how milk enters the coconut? When all this is over, Piniki, I would like to talk to your aunt, Konono, about her daughter Poro.

Piniki: Yes, mother of all children, your prayer is our hope for the future. Just go through Mojiriemu, her aunt who is already close friends with Clark's mother, Umukoko and you have reached the heart of Amakashe, her father. I believe they are all now at Amatolo.

Mitovwodo: Quarter or town?

Piniki: They could be in either place, Ma'am.

Mitovwodo: Clever people!

Branuvwere: Oh, I want to live many many floods more so that I can catch fish here to distribute among a fresh wave of children. Children are fruits of joy, children are a working team, children are a force to defend the family. Did you see how Okorugbo, James, Ogedegbe with all the younger ones, male and female, closed round their father, and drove back that horde of Kiagbodo people that had already started rejoicing that the great shark was in the net?

Mitovwodo: So, Kiagbodo people were already out dancing?

Piniki: A people who do not accept a leader are lost forever.

Branuvwere: (*spitting in disgust*) Uyo, Olomuoro, and of course, the Babigha clan, were all out there, calling for vengeance to the other bank of the river in the name of their evil gods, burnt down by Bekederemo.

Mitovwodo: (*breaking into song and dance*)

> The shield that God forged for Osio
> Is never, never to fall
> Oh yes, how ever slippery the ground
> Never, never will he fall!

Piniki: Not so loud, not so loud, Madam, white people, you know, don't like a noise.

Branuvwere: Which white men - the ones who are already dancing there with the girls? There, listen!

(*Sound of drumming and singing pouring from the compound.*)

VI

Briefing

Lagos. At the Office of the Governor-General and Commander-in-Chief of the new British Protectorate of Nigeria, Government House, Marina.

Principal Secretary: Does His Excellency really want to see this chief from Warri? I refer to the minutes. I mean, from all indications, especially from the reports by Resident Douglas and Major Wood before, it seems the man is a difficult character.

Colonel Moorhouse: Yes?

P.S: He seems to be of the class of Tietie of Kakpra - Kakprame.

Colonel Moorhouse: Must be Ikakpamre. The man was deported, if I remember correctly, to Calabar, after fighting a duel with Major Crawford. Real tongue twisters they have for names. But anthropologists Talbot here and Meek on the Benue inform us that every name, be it of place or person, tells a story of the tribe. So it is always good to try and call them correctly for these are a proud people.

P.S: Yes, Sir.

Colonel Moorhouse: You were making the point –

P. S: Yes, Sir, I was saying Chief Bagadermo –

Colonel Moorhouse: Bekederemo, you mean; it is a fuller name, a mouthful, if I recollect correctly – I knew him fairly well.

P. S: He seems to me, Sir, to belong to the class of chiefs we cannot fully trust with our programme of pacification, although appointed Warrant Chief by Copeland - Crawford. While not quite like that woman Gbetinere of Kpokpo, who Chief Dore reports stoutly refuses to assist in the war effort against the Axis Powers, he certainly strikes me as a troublesome character.

Colonel Moorhouse: Well, as for our war effort, let's refresh our minds again, before the Chief comes calling, with some of the other reports we have on him.

P. S: Here, Sir, the heading is:

"Warri Province Annual Report" (*date unclear, sir*).
"Reference No. 05026/2
File No. 11857 Vol. 1."

The representatives of the numerous firms informed me that there have been a fallen (*sic*) off in their cash sales. This also applied in Koko and Sapele. This is mainly accounted for by the fact that an enterprising chief and trader, Bekederemo by name, has chartered a launch viz (Bekederemo) from Messrs John Holt Company, Warri, and makes periodical trips through the creeks to Lagos selling oil and kernel there to a better advantage and purchasing for cash in Lagos clothes and other trade goods which they obtain at a very less (*sic*) price than for what they have to pay in Warri or Sapele. Although, I have not personally seen this launch on her journey, I am informed by those that have that it is worth seeing, the launch being packed with natives and goods of merchandise and towing of canoes also laden.
Signed
?
Resident"

End, Sir, of one. I can't quite decipher the signature.

Colonel Moorhouse: That could be James Davidson, Frank Hives or Brown. But no matter. Let's hear the other report there in your hand.

P.S: Of course, yes, Sir. It is the Intelligence Report, (Historical) Mein Clan, and Western Ijo Division 24 (year not quite clear) N.A. Class Mark War 149/2.

Colonel Moorhouse: That, I hazard a guess, must have been sent in by P.V. Main.

P.S: Correct, Sir, that's quite amazing - to carry all that amount of information among the great load of facts and cases His Excellency has to deal with -

Colonel Moorhouse: Just read on. You too will manage to cope in the course of time. So let's hear our anthropologist.

P.S: Heading, Sir, is "Bekedermo. 54" with one 'e' dropped out -

Colonel Moorhouse: Oh, yes, we murder most of their names in all forms, if we don't the men themselves in our push for possession of their land.

P.S: (*in horror*) Sir!

Colonel Moorhouse: How else are empires built - from Roman to our own times? Surely, they must have taught you that much at Eton and Cambridge. Come on, let's hear more about the man who wants to see us.

P.S: Yes, Your Excellency. (*He reads the report*)

"Bekedermo, a court member" –

The typing is faint here, Your Excellency –

Colonel Moorhouse: Never mind, read what you can make of it. Don't forget this is the handiwork of our support staff from Freetown and Accra. Quite commendable they are able to cope with such volume of work with so little formal education.

P.S: Yes, Sir, Your Excellency, (*He resumes reading*)

"Bekedermo, a court member...the largest trader and middleman for the Niger Company at GanaGana in this part of the river. His compound, it is thought, equals in size to that of the Oba of Benin and is surrounded by substantial brick walls. There are the two long barracks, wives houses, on either side one of which is constructed in cement. The compound also contains Bekederemo's own house, a well built and lofty building, and a rest house for Europeans. Niger Company agents...

Col. Moorhouse: That will do. Now, do you think that's the kind of native we should refuse audience?

P. S: Well, obviously, as it stands, the Lt. Governor at Ibadan could see him -

Col. Moorhouse: Come on, my good fellow. This is a native who does good business with us in the new legitimate trade in palm oil and kernel that His Majesty's Government has set out here to create into a great market, stretching from the Atlantic to the Sahara, as part of the great British Empire upon which, it is said, and I must concede, with great truth and justification, that the sun never sets. We have to see him if only in the interest of promoting our war effort, as you so correctly put it.

P. S: In the clear light that H. E. has put it, we'll put in motion immediately all appropriate action as Your Excellency has directed.

Col. Moorhouse: Not just my wish, my good fellow. It's good policy. This is a man Lord Leverhulme himself and the Lever brothers visit from time to time with great profit to us, in the course of our mission to pacify the natives, and make them a productive people. Furthermore, look at who he is bringing with him, the lawyer, Egerton Shyngle, leader of the Nigerian bar. Imagine the additional political rumpus and flak it will cause were we to refuse the Chief audience. The nationalist press will pick it up like a dog grabs a bone, not only here but you can be sure the anti-imperialist press at home. Next, there will be questions asked here at Leg. Co. and even in Parliament for which we shall have the unpleasant duty of providing the Secretary of State for the Colonies with plausible, I mean, acceptable answers.

P.S: Now, I fully understand, Your Excellency. An appropriate reply will go to Mr. Egerton Shyngle approving of the visit by Chief Beke...

Col. Moorhouse: Ambakederemo, now I remember. That's the man's full name. Now, you may go.

P. S: Yes, Your Excellency. Just one other matter -

Col. Moorhouse: Later, later. Remember Mrs. Moorhouse expects us home early today to go to the Polo Club. The Sultan, I gather, has come from Sokoto with quite a team of thoroughbreds, I wouldn't be surprised if not brought all the way from Saudi Arabia.

P.S: Yes, Sir, of course, Your Excellency. How could I have forgotten such an important engagement.

Col. Moorhouse: And do not forget, in this business of ruling the natives, we must always let them believe we are their humble, most obedient servants.

P.S.: Yes, Your Excellency!

(He rushes out, while H.E. lights his pipe)

VII

Audience

The same, some days after. Opening in the reception room, the action moves into the main office.

P.S: His Excellency, the Governor - General and Commander-in-Chief of the Armed Forces of the Colony of Lagos and the Protectorate of Nigeria, is pleased to receive the Chief from Warri Province.

Shyngle: Now, Chief, please remember what we said; it is the highest administrator of the land you are visiting.

Bekederemo: Don't you worry, my friend, it is not how you drink water you drink soup.

(*Both Chief and lawyer are ushered into the main office from the far end of which the great colonial officer, seated behind his large desk, graciously rises to meet the native chief*)

Col. Moorhouse: (extending his hand) Hello, my dear Chief Bekederemo, how good to see you again.

Bekederemo: (*refusing to shake hands*) Are you not Col. Moorhouse?

Col. Moorhouse: Yes, of course, my dear Chief.

Bekederemo: The Lt. Governor, Southern Provinces, Ibadan?

Col. Moorhouse: That is correct, that is, until lately, Chief Bekederemo.

Bekederemo: Then what are you doing here? Where is the Governor-General, Sir Frederick Lugard?

Shyngle: Chief Bekederemo, you promised –

Col. Moorhouse: No, Mr. Shyngle, let the Chief go on.

Bekederemo: I have not come to see you, Col. Moorhouse. If I had wanted to, I would have gone to Ibadan. I came to see Sir Frederick Lugard, the Governor-General –

Shyngle and P.S (*almost together*) Good Lord, Chief, I told you –
Good heavens, Your Excellency, I said –

Col. Moorhouse: No, no, I said let the good Chief finish.

Bekederemo: I said I did not come to see you, Colonel Moorhouse. I came to see the Governor-General.

P.S: His Excellency is the Officer Administering the Government of Nigeria in the absence of Sir Frederick Lugard, the Governor-General, now on home leave in the United Kingdom, after a long tour in these unhealthy parts.

Bekederemo: Come, Shyngle, I am going. I did not come for this.

Shyngle: This is how they regularly arrange things – it is the system – the next officer in the chain of command acting for the superior when he is away. So I plead with you, present your petition to His Excellency.

Bekederemo: Are you my lawyer or theirs?

P.S: Your Excellency, this is too much. I advised against this visit, you will remember.

Bekederemo: Are you coming? I do not expect justice at the hand of this man. He is the friend and patron of Dore Numa against whom I have come to lodge complaints, not just personal ones, but from representatives of all peoples in Warri Province.

Col. Moorhouse: Calm down, Chief Bekederemo, please calm down. I stand here not as the Colonel Moorhouse that you know but as His Majesty's officer duly appointed to administer this country, while the substantive holder of the office, Sir Frederick Lugard, is away on home leave. We uphold the same law. So you can safely present to me the petition that you have for him. On my word of honour as an officer, and more so, one charged as Officer Administering the Government, I assure you of fair and full hearing of your case.

Shyngle: Listen, please, Chief, listen to His Excellency's offer, and be assured of due process.

Bekederemo: Can I truly get justice from you, Colonel Moorhouse, after all you have done to us in favour of your agent and friend?

Col. Moorhouse: Trust me, Chief, trust me. We have come here to establish the rule of law, not to favour or fear anybody. We have no permanent friends. It is true we appointed Chief Dore Numa our Political Agent for Benin and Warri Rivers for his services to the crown in Ebrohimi and Benin. It is true thereafter he served as a member of all our patrols and expeditions in your part of the Niger Delta, taking part in the Kwale Patrol of 1906, following the murder on active duty of District Commissioner Reginald William Bird, the Abbi Rising of 1910, the Oweh Patrol, and what must have touched you most of all, the two Ijaw Patrols of 1911, following the murder of D.C. Henry James, Forcados, at Adagbabiri –

Bekederemo (*interrupting*): What about Odi you had earlier destroyed to the ground the year you attacked Nana? What about Kuno –?

Moorhouse: (*cutting in in his turn*): Oh yes, you could say we have had quite a catalogue of campaigns against some difficult tribes in the course of creating your country Nigeria, and for their services we have awarded medals to men like Chief Dore.

Bekederemo: You then set him up as President, Warri Native Court of Appeal and sent him here as Member, Nigeria Council. Now he parades himself as Paramount Ruler, Olu of Itsekiri, Sobos and Ijaws, leasing other people's land to Government without the owner's knowledge and consent.

Shyngle: This is the heart of the petition that Chief Bekederemo has brought on behalf of the people of Warri Province and himself.

Bekederemo: There are more charges –

Col. Moorhouse: I expect so, Chief. Now, shall we take them one by one? So, Chief, if you will care to sit down, we shall listen to you in full, and I promise you British justice.

Bekederemo: All right, all right.

Col. Moorhouse: And Mr. Shyngle, is that the petition the Chief has brought on behalf of himself and his people against Chief Dore?

Shyngle: Yes, Your Excellency. Every charge and complaint is fully documented here. The man is a tyrant, and, if I may venture to add, a poor choice to promote your policy of indirect rule.

Col. Moorhouse: Let me have it. (*He takes the petition, steers Chief Bekederemo and Mr. Shyngle to their seats, sits himself opposite them, and begins to go through the document in a deliberate manner.*) I see, I see. So you've got hold of the Pretheroe Report on how we moved out the Ogbe-Ijoh people to build the new township of Warri–

P.S.: But that's official classified secret information!

Col. Moorhouse: (*still thumbing through the pages of the petition*) These people have their own devices. Yes, I see, I see.

Bekederemo: Colonel Moorhouse, you have not seen all. You are in fact the cause of our latest problem.

Col. Moorhouse: I, Colonel Moorhouse, the cause of your latest problem?

Shyngle: If I may come in here, Your Excellency, recently as Secretary, Southern Provinces, Ibadan, you directed Douglas, the Resident, the Commissioner, Warri, to report on and, I quote, "the subject of the unification of the Jekri and Sobo tribes and the possibility of re-establishing the ancient Jekri Kingdom".

Col. Moorhouse: Yes, I remember such an idea was floated -

Bekederemo: Look, my mother's father Ofiagbere is Itsekiri - a direct descendant of Oshoron, in whose memory I give all my children Itsekiri names. So I should know. No such hybrid kingdom ever existed as Dogho is trying to sell to you.

Shyngle: Your Excellency, it took a submission from District Officer J. Davidson, Forcados, to H.M. Douglas, Commissioner, Warri, to convince Government the proposal would not work. Permit me to quote the relevant portion on page nine of our presentation: "The re-constitution of the Olu (or Alaja)" he wrote, "and the Ojeyes (who were councillors not viceroys) may tend to keep the tribe together, though it must be borne in mind that when we first took over the country, we did not find a kingdom." Paragraph, Your Excellency. And the memo goes to make the memorable point, and with your permission, Sir, I quote again, "the two tribes will no more mix than will oil and water."

Bekederemo: Except by force of fire. That is the bitter Izon truth. Now, do you really believe this your new market of unnumbered sheds that you call Nigeria will actually hold and for how long?

Col. Moorhouse: It seems it is I, not Chief Dore Numa, now on trial here.

Shyngle: Certainly, not, Your Excellency, far from it. We are just trying to spotlight some of the points in the petition of our client.

Bekederemo: The latest, we hear, is that the man has sent to you an urgent appeal to save him from Agbassa people and Okere people, whose lands he now admits through his lawyer that he leased to you without their consent and knowledge. That is how he is carrying on in Warri.

Shyngle: Indeed the point has been made by William Moore, himself an Itsekiri, to Rutherford, the Resident, Warri, that, and I quote "the position of Dore is indeed great, for a native chief to rule a Resident."

Bekederemo: The young man put it like a nut in a shell.

Col. Moorhouse: All right, all right, Chief Bekederemo. These are grave matters raised here. I assure you we shall look at them thoroughly and with sympathy.

Bekederemo: When? When will you look at them? This is not the first time these matters have been raised. You are always calling one meeting or another, setting up one committee after another, never taking any decision, while your agent runs all over the place like a buffalo.

Col. Moorhouse: Not this time, I solemnly assure you on behalf of His Majesty's Government. A visitation of high officials will come immediately to Warri to examine the matter on the spot. Will you be prepared to appear in person to present your case?

Bekederemo: Have I come all this way to ask for justice, and you ask whether I shall be at home to face Dore and Douglas with my charges?

Col. Moorhouse: I take that back, my dear Chief. But you came in your own ship, I presume.

Bekederemo: I don't travel on my own ship as a matter of principle. I ordered a yacht of the class of "Gongola" or

"Katsina", flag ships of the Niger Company, but all I got for my hard cash was a mere cargo boat.

P.S: But those are of the class of "The Ivy" and "Valiant".

Bekederemo: Colonel Moorhouse, tell your youngman I have dozens of sons of his age, and one day some of them will learn all your tricks.

Shyngle: The Chief came by sea on the "SS Falaba" at his own expense, surely a great sacrifice for his people, taking into account his entourage. And if I may add, Your Excellency knows better than us the danger of torpedoes fired by German U-boats now approaching these waters.

Col. Moorhouse: Never mind, never mind, no harm was meant. It is agreed that a panel of senior officers will come from the Governor-General's Office here in Lagos to Warri anytime from now and that the Chief himself will be there with his people to present these grave allegations made here in this petition against Chief Dore Numa. Chief, I wish you safe journey back on the "S.S. Falaba". It's from Burutu you will take your boat home to Kiagbodo, I presume?

Bekederemo: No, on my *okolada*, with my own crew, never again as part of any regatta. The boat is strictly for trade after the trick played on me by your people. I paid good money for it, cash down, if you must know.

Col. Moorhouse: Yes, unfortunately, these things do happen - even among the best of business partners. (*Chuckling, Colonel Moorhouse, Officer Administering the Government of Nigeria steers out Chief Bekederemo and his lawyer Mr. Shyngle*)

IX

Rite of Broom

At Kiagbodo, in the great hall of Bekederemo, overlooking his beach. He is brooding, seated under the arch of the entrance facing the river.

Nemugha: (*with the help of his walking stick, takes the steps into the hall*) So there you are, sitting all alone in your great hall.

Bekederemo: (*rises to meet him and settle him down on a seat beside him*) Mitovwodo will not let me rest in my own compound.

Nemugha: So you have come here to hold conversation with the fish of the river.

Bekederemo: Sometimes I wonder whether a life in exile wouldn't be a good thing after all.

Nemugha: You told me Nana and the Oba of Benin, and, I believe, you also mentioned the man from Opobo, I mean Jaja, and King Perekule of Bonny were all allowed company of the wives and relatives that they wanted to take with them.

Bekederemo: Oh, the worry of wives and children!

Nemugha: Yes, the more when they are so many! But you wouldn't want to leave behind Lakumo, Erhurunreki and Obire, if she was still alive. And of course, like two trees grown into each other, you would stand side by side with your Mitovwodo.

Bekederemo: That woman has not mellowed with age.

Nemugha: And have you? I wonder what you will be at my age.

Bekederemo: I know she was my sole mate in my boat, when I was coming to this world. All that crowd out there just scrambled aboard, when they saw a great enterprise setting out.

Nemugha: Even Lakumo, Obire and –

Bekederemo: Oh, life is not all business.

Nemugha: Yes, one wants to escape the rigour of work from time to time.

Bekederemo: There I was receiving accounts from agents reporting from all my produce stations in preparation to go to Ganagana, especially now the white man has introduced new methods of payment, but this woman wouldn't let me absorb the details of a trade changing everyday before our very eyes.

Nemugha: I hear they came as usual from Kakpamre, Otujevwen, Imode, Efronto, Orere, Oviri Olomu, Okunbiri, Eghwu, Odokpokpo, Agbarha-Otor -

Bekederemo: You mock me, my elder.

Nemugha: Oh, no no no, mock you, for looking after me and crowds of others! The account, however, must be correctly stated, all that tonnage of casks of oil and bags of kernel, ready for exchange for cash or barter with the white merchants at Ganagana and Warri in return for textile, tobacco, drinks, biscuits, crockery - and of course, when you arrive in port, all the other traders must step aside for you or sell out to you. I hear the cranes themselves cry out under the weight of so many casks of oil that they have to lift.

Bekederemo: Now, old man, I know in my reckless youth you saved my life, when my father almost drowned me in a boat upturned, for betting with Siake, his grand daughter –

Nemugha: There, somebody's bowels are beginning to boil over with no fire lit under them.

Bekederemo: I don't have to be told that in the end I shall carry nothing away with me. The boat will return empty, with no soul mate, crew and passengers.

Nemugha: No, no, I did not say that.

Bekederemo: Yes, yes, that was what you meant, crab that you are, always circling round your subject. But that woman sometimes pushes her position too far. There can be only one captain in a ship, giving the orders.

Nemugha: Not like the one you gave today. Yeast in the wine of others takes time to rise; with you it is straight to the top at the serving. Was this not the girl you once married off to some Niger Company manager? Indeed, she was one of the first girls to ride a bicycle in these parts. Now, you are giving her away to a complete stranger from Kolokuma, or is it Akassa?

Bekederemo: Is a man from Kolokuma or Akassa not as good as one from Bristol or Liverpool?

Nemugha: There you are right. I admit Kalabari and Brass are not the end of the world. After all, don't the young and strong of our town rush off to Tuon every fishing season?

Bekederemo: Aminose is my daughter, free for me to marry off to any man I approve.

Nemugha: Without even knowing who the gentleman is, and where he comes from?

Bekederemo: We give our daughters away in marriage to white men, knowing not where they come from, and that every two, three years, they will go back home to their first wives.

Nemugha: That is a practice your mother's people have adopted and perfected as state policy.

Bekederemo: It is a policy that serves them well; one needs allies to secure power or at least influence those who have it.

Nemugha: What have you gained by giving away your daughter to a stranger with such a name as Fenatangbe: Tie-up-and-throw-away? I'm afraid your wife is right in crying that you have cast away her daughter.

Bekederemo: I also gave away Temagha to a man from the same Sagbama Creek, but her mother made no protest.

Nemugha: She's crying silently in her room, wringing her hands so hard that blood could pour out of them like water from a wet dress.

Bekederemo: Those men you call strangers came all the way here to offer me their labour without asking for any pay. They are not slaves but freeborn Izon men from near our own Ugobiri.

Nemugha: But Fenatangbe - what a name! What is your other new son-in-law called?

Bekederemo: Now, what's his name?

Nemugha: There, you don't even know his name!

Bekederemo: I know it; it'll come back. Anyway, I have given my word, given directives for their canoes to be loaded with all they need to set up house, and for each of my daughters, I have provided one of my own wives to see that they are properly settled down in their new homes, and then, they can come back to report to me.

Nemugha: The chaperons will see only the sowing of the seeds in the soil. What manner of plants will spring up only time will tell. There is a story budding there that luckily I shall not be around to hear.

Bekederemo: You were for ever the wall-gecko.

Nemugha: That's right, never venturing out. That's why we remain stunted here in one place. Now, now look up there. Do I see the sister you also generously gave away to your Itsekiri friend, when you were just setting out?

Bekederemo: Fiobode, my sister!

Fiobode: (*Walking in with her heavy gait and kneeling, first to her brother who hugs her closely, then to the old man, laughing quietly to himself*). My knees are on the ground; I'm kneeling down.

Nemugha: (*commenting on her gait*) Young woman, did you walk all the way from Warri?

Bekederemo: It's those feet of your friend. He gave them to all of us.

Nemugha: Tut, tut, tut! It's her husband who could not put her in a proper carriage.

Fiobode: Not so, Sir. I have come with my usual train. I wanted in fact to come by water. But I missed my brother's boat, because it was off-loading at Ovwian and Aladja passengers from Lagos. How is everybody here at home, the wives, the children –?

Bekederemo: Oh, go there and see how your wife the elder has turned my compound into a market that a masquerade has scattered. Right now, I hear she's gone crying for her sons to fight me.

Fiobode: What does she want now, the one you tell all the world is your bread and potato?

Bekederemo: Cassava, my sister.

Nemugha: Fiobode, never mind your brother. There is nothing happening that we haven't seen before.

Fiobode: Those children were always violent; fortunately, the younger one, Okemeji, has gone to his world. You remember when he spat at my brother –

54

Nemugha: What a thoughtless thing to say! Fiobode, you haven't come home to add oil to a fire that you haven't even seen. That incident, everybody knew later, was the first sign, the symptom of the illness that was to take him to his early and sad end.

Bekederemo: Oh, let's not dig up unhappy stories of our past. This is my one sister who cares for me.

Nemugha: While away in Warri running her husband? And Onotanarien, your youngest, is even farther away at Age by the sea. You're unfair to Yenke, who's here with you all the time.

Bekederemo: When is she here with me? She spends all her time now with that man Suoware who is not worth one of the fingers on my left hand. *Bah*, a woman of her age and position, oh, she has truly shamed me for all Kiagbodo to laugh at. So you don't believe me? Send to her now, and if you find her at home, I'll send you a carton of any drink that you care to call for.

Nemugha: A relationship that has yielded us a fine daughter like Orukepriye, what else do we want from it?

Bekederemo: She is seen every night slipping to his quarters, if he is not the one stealing into her bed. A woman of her age and station, still wanting sex. Come, Fiobode, tell me what is going on in Warri. I've been waiting for word from Douglas about the delegation coming from Lagos.

Fiobode: Oh, my dear, dear brother, that is why I have come.

Bekederemo: What has it got to do with you?

Fiobode: My husband sent me to you to say the officers have come and gone.

Bekederemo: (*springing to his feet*) Come and gone?

Fiobode: Yes, my brother, they have come and gone.

Bekederemo: When?

Fiobode: Only yesterday. My husband and his brother Shimishere, the one who calls himself Mr. Skin, came back from their meeting very agitated. Everybody in the compound could see they were in a state of shock. Dore had just announced to them with great fanfare that the big white people, who you went all the way to Lagos to summon to try him, had come and gone, after seeing the Resident and himself. He said that they didn't even bother to ask for you.

Bekederemo: Colonel Moorhouse promised me justice – British justice.

Fiobode: From what my husband and his brother said, it seems they told the delegation that they had sent several times for you, but that in your haughtiness and stubbornness, you refused to answer their call.

Nemugha: When the man went all the way to Lagos, are they saying he couldn't find the time and the energy to go to Warri, a few tides away, to present his case and witnesses?

Fiobode: That's exactly what my husband and everybody in Warri are asking. They are all saying that the white men from Lagos did not believe the story, but that they had to take what their man on the spot told them.

Bekederemo: And the officers from Lagos believed this lie? That is the part I do not want to accept. As for Douglas and Dore, they are twins in perfidy, although God made them of different colours.

Fiobode: My husband says I must tell you all is not lost. Mr. Alders, the interpreter, no, the Court Clerk, Mr. Bar-Rolle, later told them in confidence that Dore has been stripped of many of his powers by the high officers from Lagos. Each group of people in the province is now to run its own affairs, conduct its own courts, send a member to the court of appeal –

Bekederemo: That's enough! I don't want to hear any more.

Nemugha: What about the people whose lands he gave away to the white man, without their knowledge and consent? Are they going to get them back?

Fiobode: Deep is the river of bad blood he has dug between our people. I swim in it everyday in Warri, coming to it in full flood from all three sources. And nobody knows when this unnatural flood will ebb.

Bekederemo: Yes, there are troubled waters ahead - in this our land flowing with oil. Dore did not just set out to sell other people; in his self-serving career with the white man he has thoroughly compromised his own people, my mother's people. Does he really believe the white man will always be here to hold his hand?

Nemugha: You told our king and council, when the white man first came among us, I think the man MacDonald, no, Tubman Goldie, was the first to steam into these waters, that we should accept to trade with him, but as for settling among us as arbiter in our affairs about which he knows nothing, we should show him some other places to go. That's why they went and set up shop at Ganagana on the main river, and in Okpare and Umolo upstream on our creek. See the confusion he has since brought us, by forcing an unequal union upon peoples with different tongues, customs and traditions, and as if that was not enough, he sets his chosen servant to preside over us. Does the man Dore speak Izon, Urhobo, Isoko or Kwale that he adjudicates our cases? A stranger has big eyes but he doesn't see the ways of his hosts.

Bekederemo: The white man must always have one black man he can trust to do his purpose, and he will reward his chosen one out of all proportion, if only to punish his compatriots and peers for refusing to serve his cause.

Nemugha: That's why he is now ruling the world. He uses the conquered against themselves. And as we have seen, what he lays his hands on, he holds on to like a gorilla.

Fiobode: I am so afraid. Suddenly the world has become a fearful place.

Nemugha: It was always so, my dear girl, it has always been so. The white man has merely made it more of a mess for us. Fortunately, I shall not be around much longer to swim in it.

Bekederemo: But your children's children and mine will be.

Fiobode: God help us! Oh, what a world! What a life!

Bekederemo: (*biting his forefinger, as he paces up and down, suddenly looks up, his eyes burning bright*) A broom, Fiobode, get me a broom.

Fiobode: A broom? My brother, what will you do with a broom?

Bekederemo: I said get me a broom. There – in that corner!

Fiobode: Yes, of course, as you want it, my brother, more dear to me, more precious to me than anything in the world. (*She goes and fetches the broom from one corner of the great hall, where it had been left forgotten by some cleaner, and hands it to her brother with both hands*).

Bekederemo: (*Takes the broom from her with his left hand, and bending down, with ritual flourish, begins to sweep the floor in the direction of the main entrance, facing the river*) Whisk! Whisk! Whisk! Thus, with my left hand, I sweep away the life of Dore. May his life go out with all his minions he placed in all courts to preside in Izon, in Urhobo, in Isoko, in Kwale, in Aboh, and even in his own Itsekiri land, yes, everywhere the white man has overpaid him for the dirty services he has done against his own people. Whisk! Whisk! Whisk! May Dore's life go out like the puff of a foul wind. May it evaporate like the mist when the sun rises. May he leave behind no seed to increase the tree of his life. May his line end with his career, built upon the suffering of all living in these rivers. May his name be remembered only for the treachery and perfidy he perpetrated against the land of his birth. Thus, with my left hand, I sweep away the life of Dore as common dust. Whisk! Whisk! Whisk! (*He throws out the broom and spits after it*). That is my curse this day of the man before God.

IX

Sickbed

On the porch of Bekederemo's main house at the far end of his compound with only Tamarasan, his Altar to the Almighty, between it and the guest rest house towards the front gate. He is sitting back in a reclining chair adjusted to a half-sitting position. Mitovwodo is sitting beside him, and Piniki singing to him.

Piniki:

>When we hadn't even quarrelled
>Iko would up and say
>If I but sing a song
>Osio's wives will all pack and go
>As things would happen
>It's Iko who is now left alone in bed
>God truly does his will
>The hippopotamus spouts
>It spits on its own head.

(*Piniki repeats the song*)

Bekederemo: My Lady of Cassava, haven't we come a long way? The battles that you and I have seen since, as almost boy and girl, commoner and princess ran away together to Ayagha.

Mitovwodo: Don't talk so much, it is not good for your condition. We know that where we are going now is shorter than where we came from, and the energy is not as before. But whatever battle lies in front, we shall meet it together.

Bekederemo: Perhaps in our running feud with the house of Babigha, we dealt with the old man a little too hard. I hope some of our offspring to come will staunch the wounds now bleeding between us. After all, teeth and tongue have achieved accommodation in a small space.

Mitovwodo: Their gods called for destruction. Okporuaro would have beaten his calabash around town calling you a coward, after you swore to king and council that you will rid the town of a great curse. It was a day to live or die.

Bekederemo: Spoken like the good partner that you've always been to me. But I think we should be building bridges before going. I called my elder sister today to prepare to die before I go, and she clapped her hands full in my face.

Mitovwodo: That was a fearful thing to ask of anyone.

Bekederemo: You know all I want is her safety and happiness. Her suffering will be great, when I go before her. It is true death observes no order of precedence, but I have grave fears for my sister, Yenken, when I'm gone.

Mitovwodo: But you aren't going anywhere yet. This is not the first time that you have been gravely ill or close to death in battle. God has always brought you back from the other shore. Look, when your half brother Sabolo shot you in the chest with his double barrel gun in front of everybody, did you die? When Dore sent you an ark loaded with small pox, did you not float it right back to him so that in the end, it was that evil man who had to sacrifice bullocks to his ancestors against all custom to save himself. In the matter of the twins at Agbodobri, when all the town reported you to Dore and his white friends for committing multiple murder, did Erekebena your wife, her father and entire family not absolve you of the charge? And where is Uyo of Amatolo today, who never let you forget you are the son of a daughter on both sides in Kiagbodo, and therefore must go and settle at Okpokunu and Tebegbe or even go to Ugbokoto, your mother's father's place? Today, he has fled to Akotogbo near the Ilaje, never to come back.

Bekederemo: Well, as a gambler in my youth, I know I have had my fair share of good luck. But on that day the hand changes for the worst, I hope I shall be ready to take it.

Mitovwodo: You have started again.

Bekederemo: A man must be ready to go, knowing how he came. Indeed, at our last count, the bamboo and cane in the loft were already complete and turned to gold.

Mitovwodo: It is a dreadful habit for a man to have, collecting the parts for his own coffin.

Bekederemo: The good paddler looks after his canoe.

Mitovwodo: So you have gone and instilled this terrible practice in your son.

Bekederemo: And I hope he passes it on to his son.

Mitovwodo: I don't like it at all. For a man who came in a vessel festooned for the sun, you have a strange way of calling the wet day.

Bekederemo: Now, aren't I rain myself!

Mitovwodo: That's a prayer to temper the sun, and loosen the earth. But everybody knows you are fire.

Bekederemo: Right now, I am all ember and ashes.

Mitovwodo: God forbid it. There, let me fan you.

Bekederemo: But if you should fail to fan me back to life, tell Fiobode and Fuludu they must not let Kiagbodo and clan know I am gone, until they have washed me, rubbed me all over with sap of camwood, and covered me in my black shroud of calico. Only then may my family weep as loud as they say I wept for my mother so that the public at large can come to the show, that we know, so many of them have prayed for, for years.

Mitovwodo: I will not sit here to hear any more of this.

Bekederemo: There, sit down, and then fan me as much as you like, since you and I know that you blow as much for me as for yourself. As it is, my parents are old enough to bear me again. Oh, what is there to life in this world?

Mitovwodo: Yes, life fills one with fear. But what can we do? In daylight we are in darkness.

Piniki (*singing*)

> Oh, mother, have faith
> Oh, Koko, have faith
> The fight we fear would kill Ikhimi
> That's the one that brings him home safely.

Mitovwodo: Sing that song again, Piniki, sing it again, so that your master can hear his own words.

Bekederemo: I hear them all right, Mitovwodo, and my state of mind and body asks for the song. But you and I know very well that the body is no longer what it was. Look, I can't even tell whether it is illness of the flesh, a lowness of spirit, or just the body in sheer fatigue. My legs are heavy as if weighted down with chains and they have the coldness of iron which some say is the beginning of the end. Not through the heart and the head, but the feet does death enter the body. Yes, legs were the special problem of my father's. Can a condition like that be passed down from father to son?

Mitovwodo: Come, take your medicine, and stop all this nonsense talk. It is a well-known fact that children pick all sorts of things from their parents, most of the time not necessarily the best attributes.

Bekederemo: Oh, my father was really special. When the general, who fought so many battles for this same ungrateful Kiagbodo, even against his father's town, Okpokunu, lost the power of his lower half, you remember what he did. Against all customs and tradition, he settled his young wives he approved of among his selected sons.

Mitovwodo: You have no cause to follow in his footsteps.

Bekederemo: And you have no cause to fear you'll suffer a similar fate. Beautiful as you are to me still, you are a grandmother several times over. Moreover, between Fuludu and his Ogiogio royal house, I won t have to drag on long like the old warrior, demanding company every day and night.

Mitovwodo: And he would insist on eating at least six times a day. I wonder where he put it all. After that, it was his pipe he would fight ceaselessly to stuff with tobacco all in one piece. God save the wife who brought him a dish he took instant dislike to. Only that girl Umukoko won his commendation. Then he would roar for you, son that he spent so much time to whip onto the right path, to send him another case of tobacco before he had hardly worked his way up the sheaf of tobacco.

Bekederemo: Yes, old age is a terrible thing, the ever growing disease that man suffers to the end. But listen, if my ears are not just ringing, I believe I hear some noise out there. What is Kiagbodo up to again? (*husband and wife listen together, and indeed there seems to be a rush of women and children to the gate. As Piniki offers to go and find out the cause of the commotion outside, Branuvwere hobbles in*).

Mitovwodo: What is it, old man?

Branuvwere: A dreadful thing, Bekederemo, a dreadful thing.

Bekederemo: Have crocodiles crawled ashore? I thought I had cleared them out of our rivers after they killed two of my daughters.

Branuvwere: It is worse than that, I can't say it with my mouth.

Bekederemo: Well, shall we send for pen and paper then for you to write it down, stark illiterates that we all are?

Branuvwere: It is Fetaroro –

Bekederemo and Mitovwodo: (*together*) That man! What is he up to again?

Branuvwere: All got up like a real apparition, he is heading straight for here.

Mitovwodo: For here? And what did the men of Kante do — Odjegbu, Odidimako, Egbucha, Okoro?

Branuvwere: None of your strong men dared come near him.

Bekederemo: And the women of Indibeye — Kpekpeyi, Okuboye, Madase, Ekpughele ?

Branuvwere: None, none could touch him. By now he must have passed your father's compound.

Mitovwodo: And Orogen, Zetu, Akpowei, Iyagua — none could stop the wizard?

Branuvwere: Ogedegbe has ordered the gates locked, and only James with his one eye, has mounted the roof ready to shoot at the apparition.

Mitovwodo: Where are all the other men of this compound that knows no sleep? Oh, sad that Fuludu has gone back to Patani! And Okemeji dead!

(*A gun shot is heard outside, then a bell ringing over and above the din*).

Bekederemo: (*sitting up*) Let the man in. He wants to see me, not so? Let him. Tell Ogedegbe to open the gates.

Branuvwere: Oh, what a day! There, the snake has slunk in! (*The unwanted visitor, in a red skull cap and skirt, bell in one hand and horse tail in the other, has gained entrance into the compound, and is now cavorting about the place, everybody running away from him*).

Bekederemo: Here I am, Fetaroro, here I am! I don't remember sending for you after burning down your evil outfit.

Fetaroro: Yes, you didn't invite me.

Bekederemo: Then, what are you doing in my compound?

Fetaroro: I had to come. It's Ngbile our father, who sent me to you.

Bekederemo: Did you also see our ancestor as you saw your evil spirits in your dreams?

Fetaroro: Do not make light of matters of the spirit, Bekederemo. You have walked over our gods, humbled my father, family and district. So I should have no cause to bring you any message to cheer your heart. It is a message none of your soothsayers can bring you, not even Rewane from your mother's side, yes, believe me, not even Rewane.

Bekederemo: You people lament the loss of your collection as if you were orphans. If I set fire to your wicked gods, I also consigned mine to water. Only my altar to our Creator stands between me now and all forces outside.

Fetaroro: We poor ones still rely on ours. Though you uproot them from our town, they are raising their heads right now in other places - Erhuwanren, Okpare, Aladja, Orhughwerun and soon I shall install them at Okpavuerhe, although against all omens warning me to fold in my wings.

Bekederemo: So, what have you come to tell me?

Fetaroro: I said Ngbile sent me. Our ancestor has revealed to me in a vision that I must come to you, braving men and weapons on the way.

Bekederemo: And what is your message from our ancestor so great that you have broken all barriers to reach me?

Fetaroro: You will not die.

Bekederemo: Liar! Of course, I shall die -

Fetaroro: Not of this illness; you will not die of this illness that so many doctors have come from every direction of the wind to cure. Our father says there is still work for you to do here and beyond for our people. Never mind the people of Kiagbodo. Your mission reaches far beyond them. And when your mission here in these rivers is finished, a great tornado will come upon this land, and then, in spite of all the walls of brick you build around yourself, your life will go out with that oil lamp you have set up to burn for ever there in front of your altar to our Creator. Now I go back to lowly Kpakabiri and Apono from where I came. I came not to seek war with Pobolo. Our problems are many but they lie outside.

Bekederemo: Fetaroro, you know life is only a bubble made by a paddle in the river. We see ourselves large in it, but it bursts in our face before we know it.

Fetaroro: And we also know the deepest track we make here on earth, and call our career, is no more than the wake a boat makes. It tears up the river with pride but the river soon swallows it up. Arrival is all, yes it is the arrival that matters.

Bekederemo: Who can grab his shadow?

Fetaroro: And who can catch his echo? So the song goes on.

Bekederemo: It is said a dance should cease when the ovation is loudest.

Fetaroro: Your song will go on as long as there is voice to sing. Now, stay well.

Bekederemo: And Fetaroro, you go well.
Fetaroro: (*breaks into song as he dances his way out*).

> When lamp goes out
> Men grope about the house
> When the sun goes down
> The earth goes to sleep.

Bekederemo: (*turning to his wife*) Have you seen such a surprise performance before?

Mitovwodo: Well, have you?

Bekederemo: And you my old teacher?

Branuvwere: Me, a poor household slave? I don't understand you Izon people.

Bekederemo: Well, this news should please my sister, Yenken.

Mitovwodo: It is honey on all our tongues, oil for our lamps in the white man's new night market he calls Nigeria.

THE END

www.ingramcontent.com/pod-product-compliance
Lightning Source LLC
Chambersburg PA
CBHW011749220426
43669CB00020B/2951